Airstream

Airstream

poems by
Audrey Henderson

HOMEBOUND PUBLICATIONS
Independent Publisher of Contemplative Titles
STONINGTON, CONNECTICUT

PUBLISHED BY HOMEBOUND PUBLICATIONS

Airstream Copyright © 2014 by Audrey Henderson. All Rights Reserved. Without limiting the rights under copyright reserved above, no part of this publication may be reproduced, stored in or introduced into a retrieval system or transmitted in any means (electronic, mechanical, photocopying, recording or otherwise) without the prior written permission of both the copyright owner and publisher except for brief quotations embodied in critical articles and reviews.

For bulk ordering information or permissions write:
Homebound Publications, PO Box 1442
Pawcatuck, Connecticut 06379 United States of America
Visit us at: www.homeboundpublications.com

FIRST EDITION
ISBN: 978-1-938846-42-7 (pbk)

BOOK DESIGN
Front Cover Image: © Sunset Airstream by Peter Galvin (Flickr)
Cover and Interior Design: Leslie M. Browning

Library of Congress Cataloging-in-Publication Data

Henderson, Audrey, 1961-
 [Poems. Selections]
Airstream / by Audrey Henderson. —First edition.
   pages cm
 ISBN 978-1-938846-42-7 (pbk.)
 I. Title.
 PS3608.E39254A6 2014
 811'.6--dc23
                                                                2014030724

10 9 8 7 6 5 4 3 2 1

Homebound Publications holds a fervor for environmental conservation. We are ever-mindful of our "carbon footprint". Our books are printed on paper with chain of custody certification from the Forest Stewardship Council, Sustainable Forestry Initiative, and the Programme for the Endorsement of Forest Certification. This ensures that, in every step of the process, from the tree to the reader's hands, that the paper our books are printed on has come from sustainably managed forests. Furthermore, each year Homebound Publications donates 1% of our annual income to an ecological or humanitarian charity. To learn more about this year's charity visit www.homeboundpublications.com.

for Richard

Acknowledgements

Grateful acknowledgements are due to the editors of the following publications where these poems first appeared:

New Writing Scotland 31, "National Library of Scotland"
Timber Creek Review, "The Elders Lament"
Taproot Literary Review, "Girls, Birds"
The Kerf, "Monarchs"
Roanoke Review, "The Big Loop"
The Sow's Ear Review, "Pueblo Birds"
The Comstock Review, "Our Fiesta"
Innisfree Poetry Journal, "St. Kilda Sunday," "Mr. Peterson's Field Guide"
FutureCycle Poetry Anthology 2012, "Airstream," "The Lichen Lovers," "A Late Encounter with the Professor of Islamic Art"
Magma, "How the Blue Nude Met the Desmoiselles"
The Midwest Quarterly, "Cobb Hill Road, 1917" "Indigo Bunting"
River Styx, "Philadelphia"
Tar River Poetry, "Dari Joy"

"Philadelphia" won 2nd place in the 2008 River Styx International Poetry Contest.

"Our Fiesta" was a Special Merit Poem in the Muriel Craft Bailey Memorial Award Contest.

"Terminus" was a Finalist in the 2008 Indiana Review 1/2K Contest.

I'm very grateful to the following people for their support, friendship and the many wise suggestions which shaped this work: Lisa Beatman, Dorothy Derifield, Elizabeth Galloway, Carolyn Gregory, Holly Guran, Susanna Kittredge, Alice Kociemba, Dorian Kostiopoulos, Jim LaFond-Lewis, Sandee Storey and Gary Whited of Jamaica Pond Poets as well as Susan Donnelly and her Tuesday group: Betty Barrer, Bob Brooks, Nellie Goodwin, Tony Majahad, Adnan Onart and Erin Trahan. To Richard, also and especially, thank you.

Contents

Acknowledgements	vii

Finisterre

The Lichen Lovers	1
Mr. Peterson's Field Guide	3
Monarchs	4
Airstream	5
St. Kilda Sunday	7
Post Card	8
The Big Loop	9
The Debt	10
The Elders Lament	11
The Ballad of Bluejohn Canyon	12
Night at Apache Pass	15
Lammermoor	17
Terminus	19
God at the Grand Canyon	21
Pueblo Birds	23

The Continent and the Levant

Goodbye Pierrot	27
How the Blue Nude Met the Demoiselles	29
The Tempest	31
National Library of Scotland	33
Hacksilber	35
A Late Encounter with the Professor	36

Heavenly Ladder of John Klimax	38
Easter, New Jersey	40
Reading Szymborska	41
From Russia	42
The Baptist	44
Shepherds	45
Syrian Grocer	46
Henri Cartier-Bresson	48
Forefathers	50
The Oases	51
Our Fiesta	52

Eastern Seaboard

Girls, Birds	57
Cobb Hill Road, 1917	58
Milledgeville	59
Fireflies	60
The Metaphysicals	61
Philadelphia	62
Mr. Elliot	64
Creatures and Beasts	65
Fledged	66
Dear Mr. Butler	67
Indigo Bunting	68
Gravity Fed	69
Morning	70
Green Valentine	71
Dari-Joy	72

About the Author
About the Press

Finisterre

The Lichen Lovers

for Sylvia Duran Sharnoff
Co-Author, Lichens of North America

What we didn't mortgage or pawn
is hardly worth mentioning.
The wedding china paid for
a specialized lens and my guitar
collection bought a motor home.
Yes, we were broke. The tongue waggers
clucked and shook their heads,
three years' carpenters wages
gone, for what? Lichen.
We gave the little speech—
sort of like moss, breaks down rock
the stuff of model railroad shrubs
and the manna that fell on God's
chosen people was a lichen actually

but we met with blank stares mostly
as we crisscrossed America
looking for clean air.
You corrected book text on your
sick bed as we reminisced
about tundra—how I shot the lichen
through a cloud of mosquitoes
while you beat the air with a glove—

and I know you loved the words,
you said it had all been worth it
to see "rock" and "tripe" juxtaposed.
Still, I wish you could tell me again
that we'd breathed in rarified air.
I wish you could tell me again
we'd eaten the bread of heaven.

Mr. Peterson's Field Guide

I've had my share
of the orange plaid settees,
the mildewed cigarette air,
the nylon sheets. Nights
as I drew pistils and spathes
in the Rob Roy Motorcourt,
the Matterhorn Lodge, I could
hear car chases through the walls.
Then there were raunchy
giggles and fumbled keys,
but these were minor distractions.
Worse were the tired salesmen
hungry for talk. I perfected excuses,
escapes—there'd be too many
questions for an old man
with a suitcase full of flowers
and I could never convey
the urgency, the need for
freshness, or the terrible way
the petals collapse.

Monarchs

We counted five monarch butterflies
going buddleia to buddleia on the way
to Mexico, via Alveston Street.
I had seen them in a National
Geographic magazine, all licking
salts and minerals with their
butterfly tongues, millions
of them, from 1967 and I thought
of a thing some scientist said
about the flap of a butterfly
wing in Tokyo affecting
the weather in Rome,
I think it was Rome,
so it's no wonder that they go
to all the trouble—that's a big
responsibility for a butterfly.
Who knows what apocalyptic
thing might happen if they
don't get to the Yucatan,
the Nile might never flood
again, the ring might slip
from Neptune.

Airstream

I want a beehive
and a Winnebago.
No, an Airstream trailer
made of aluminum
pressed into art deco rays.
I imagine the kitchens
have nickel latches
and maple doors.
I will fry us eggs in Arizona.
You will read the newspaper
as usual, on a folding chair
greyer, not bald, and eminent.
The children will be older—
Emma a scientist, Helen
something beautiful
and empathetic. We will pass
through several time zones
and see cactuses.
The trailer will shine
on the highway
like a bullet, pointed
and convex. When
we get home
I'll make us

candles
out of
yellow wax.

St. Kilda Sunday

The Reverend
tells us of kind Jesus
with the sweet gaze
and a medicine
that cures the itch.
It is true that he seems kind
although he forbids us
to tend our animals
on Sunday and I wonder
whether I can love him
more than I love
the wild thyme
where I lay my head
before I knew his name.

Post Card

The weather is perfect.
You know
how it can be on Skye
in May
and I have met someone.
We climbed
dangerous cliffs together
and on the descent
I got punch-drunk, stumbling
carelessly
through marshy ground.
I am sun-burnt.
We seem to be sharing
a small tent.
Salt water laps the pebbles
all night long.
The corncrakes are nocturnal.

The Big Loop

Spectacles
wigs and false
teeth fell from the sky.

At night
we would gather them
and wallets with medallions

organ donor cards
snap-shots of grandchildren
a single condom

because you never
know and the people
who came back

to earth, trembled
with only what their hearts
could hold.

The Debt

This morning the damp smell of cumin
and nostalgia is in the cupboard.
There's Eve with her curry of bruised
fruit and Polish Jerry with his cigarette burns.
She studied botany. I have her hairbrush,
always so careless with people's possessions.
I left my cousin's roasting pan there
and her hiking boots are still in my closet.
I wore them in the Cuillins. Now the laces
are frayed, yellow and black, like wasp bodies.
When I flew home for her funeral
my plane had a near collision with a jet.
There I was, admiring the mountain scenery
when an F16 with camouflage wings snuck
beneath our undercarriage. That's not supposed
to happen I thought as my jaw kept falling.
It was right over where I wore those boots.

The Elders Lament

At the farthest point, above the gorse and broom,
stands a stone carved with marvelous animals,
oxen, and leaping salmon, the eagle and the shape
of the new moon. On a winter morning the sun
eats clean through the cairn and the hill with light
that falls on my own stone floor. My grandmother's mirror
had the same patterns, made by the best silversmiths,
pictures of fish and deer and the great arrow. You see,
the mirror could hold my grandmother and the sky
and the entire hillside within its single gleaming eye.
After the monks arrived our most skilled stone cutters
and metalworkers built fine monuments for the new God,
giving the fruits of their craftsmanship for years,
until the elders grew silent, fearing in their hearts that no-one
would carve the stones that tether the sky to the land,
or burnish mirrors where people see their faces in the stars.

The Ballad of Bluejohn Canyon

*In 2003 Aron Ralston was trapped
by a boulder in Bluejohn Canyon, Utah.
He escaped by removing his own arm.*

It was gas
it was ghastly, me pierced
digested already,

floating away with a hiss.
That was the turning point
the turning point

when I used my blunt
pen knife, the blade dulled
by my epitaph, my RIP.

The canyon walls popped
all of them sang
with snapped bone, ulna, radius...

I was seven days shriveled
and frozen seven black nights.
Oh, the darkness...

then in the morning a single raven
every morning by eight thirty
like a tally mark...

such hard red walls.
I threw my ashes to them
I scattered my own remains

giving them to the rock.
Sinew sinew, see-saw sinew
I sliced through

myself. The raven did not
appear and I was delivered
through a cleft.

I applied a tourniquet
rappelled down a cliff
to a little pool

of sour water below.
It was septic.
There was a dead raven in it

but I drank, I drank
through feathers
and thickness I drank my fill.

Do you know how huge
the sky is, do you know
when you have been inside

the earth's split crust.
It is blue, blue blue
it is a wide gas. I was already sky.

Night At Apache Pass

All night the mountain said to me, tell them, tell them
      that our valleys were choked with bones

And the waters of our streams ran red, tell them the sighs
      of the unlamented still rise from the earth.

We brought forth the race of men from ancient days
      to praise us and marry us to the stars.

We gave them the good herb and the dark flesh of birds.
      Then all night the mountain said to me

Tell them woman, that the people with pale ancestors
      took our children in box cars.

They cut off their long hair. Our children felt the blade
      of the scissor and heard the crunch of the shear.

The barber was ankle deep in black locks and our children
      shook in chairs made of terrible metal.

All night the mountain repeated these things. Our warriors
      still guard the foothills and the high passes.

As the Chiricuahuas turn white, they look for the sign
        of the crane, listen for the sound of the season turning.

Great flocks darken the sky, descend to the plain. Tell them
        every year, fewer birds come.

Lammermoor

Tony's butcher shop is pristine—jars of tomato paste
along a shelf, jaunty cans of Pastene, the whole place
painted red and white to go with the meat. A sign in magic
marker on the cash register says bacalao $8.99 a pound.
I ask him how to cook it. When it comes out I'm from
Scotland he hands me a CD of *Lucia de Lammermoor*,
a picture of Italian men in kilts on stage at La Scala.
Tony wants to know, is it a real place, Lammermoor.
Sure it is I tell him, I could see it from my window,
but neglect to mention that it's *gey dreich* which translates
roughly into forlornest place on earth– wind swept hills
covered in heather, which blooms for five minutes
then turns a sort of off-black and there is nothing there
except the sheep, black-faced Cheviots and a Trappist
monastery whose buildings are not at pains to distinguish
themselves from a factory or detention facility. And next
to that is the cottage of my second cousin, that was Tilley's
daughter who went to art college. Tilley was a large boned
woman with a scalded appearance and the scant cork-screw
ringlets of a home permanent. The main achievement
of Tilley and her nine sisters was defeating Hitler with small
acts of thrift. They were not radical or in any way *avant
garde*, they had never heard the phrase non-traditional
family. On reflection there was only ever one comment

about the fact that Tilley's daughter set up home with
a woman and raised a wee girl up on the moor, it was that
Flora was not allowed to eat sweets. The old ladies
took it as a human rights violation, an assault on their grand-
motherly prerogative to feed her candy and would sneak
her chocolate bars on the sly, *their little secret.* Anything else
Tony asks me and I tell him, just the hamburger for now.

Terminus

I can tell you that the road is gone. I can tell you
that the houses are gone and the gas station, but you will
not understand until you step on the tarmac and it crumbles
and you will say The road is gone! The houses are gone!
Their gardens, their petunias and photographs are sucked
into the brown roar. There is no more lawn. And I need
wood to burn. Is it unseemly to pick up house timbers?
People may want to caress their house timbers, to rock
them in their arms and sing to them. Tom gives us firewood. I do not know Tom. Pam brings us sausage. I do
not know Pam. The food is warm. The end of the world
is on our doorstep. People stare at it. You cannot go
any farther, they say. No-one has information. No-one
knows whether the whole world is gone or half the world
or one millionth of it. We are solemn and gingerly by
the precipice. The night is new to us. The night is a balm.
We sit on our rooftops and wait. The stars are bluish-white
like breast milk. We count the drops falling. Do they hum
on the way down? Sleep baby. Rest your head on the hatchet.
Sleep babies. Once upon a time there was a heaven… Will
someone tell us what is happening? Someone in the next
town has a radio. Someone in the next town said Texas
is gone. Someone else said no, the polar ice cap is gone,
two pieces, twice the size of Texas. We look at the water

for answers, like the polar bear, the man from Plaquemins.
There is rumbling. There is a roar, a huge vehicle.
We admire the yellow maw, the many-angled tire,
a back hoe. The driver smiles and says didn't I just see
you in Tacloban. Didn't I see you in New Orleans?
We say No Sir. This is New Hampshire! He laughs out
loud and long. We repeat, this is New Hampshire.
He replies, still laughing, rubble is rubble, all powder
and bits of cable, nothing recognizable but the smell.

God at the Grand Canyon

I am standing at the rim of the Grand Canyon
railing at God. It's freezing and I have pajamas
on under my corduroys and one sock, which
was all I could find in the dark. "What do You
want from me?" I seethe, fulminating towards
Orion. "What do you want from me, You, God,
You?" The constellations wink back without
explanation and though there's only half a moon
the milky rocks and rockless depths loom up
in cold light. My anger does not abate. I will not
accept no answer, no explanation, this God had
better talk back. My sockless foot sticks to its insole.
Still no reply. Well, maybe gradual peace. I will
not accept gradual peace, *The Peace I Give You,
My Own Peace*. I want a response: sky-writing,
fireworks, some kind of Old Testament response,
so I say to God "I'm going to stay out here, even
if I freeze to death, until You reply, BIG TIME."

At that exact moment, a shooting star shot overhead,
a large yellow one with a long comet trail and a sort
of silent voice said "This is the work of my hand."
And it was as if a big God hand stroked the Canyon
in one gesture and at the same second as the big
hand stroking gesture, some strange singing came

up from the chasm, strange singing that was almost
discordant, yet somehow beautiful and coherent,
so that if it were a crystal, it would refract and shine
wildly, at odd angles, and although you couldn't
exactly see a pattern, you'd somehow know that there
was a complex structure nonetheless. So, this music
rose up to the sky and my hairs stood on end,
every single one, like in a comic strip and I thought
of the shepherds at Christmas, all terrified by music
coming out of the sky and the 'be not afraid' that
came with it, which I did not get, so I took theirs,
but was still, obviously, totally afraid, even though
I tried to rationalize it—campers singing Kumbaya,
coyotes howling—all the echoes fractured, disseminated
among rocks. Still, the chorus of a thousand voices
rose and while I wanted to run a mile, my feet were
rooted there until I accepted that whatever it was,
its unspeakable beauty rising out of the Canyon
into the stars couldn't be denied, not to mention
the timing, and headed back to the Bright Angel Lodge.

Pueblo Birds

I am a bad tourist.
I do not read the numbered
plaques or look for petroglyphs,
but stare at blond grasses in the sun,
the wind ruffling them to the horizon,
to the pink rock formations. I notice
that there are birds tumbling out
of the sky, sucked as by magnets
into a juniper bush and there are
more of them down the cinder path
where the air is dark with wings.
It is water that draws them—
waxwings and jays—they make
a blue as deep as the sky
by the rim of the pool.
Then they start up in clouds
and the air is thick with birds,
it is loud with the clatter
of feathers, as it has been
each year since there
was water here, and
someone drawing it
in an earthen-
ware jar.

The Continent and the Levant

Goodbye Pierrot
For Brian Diver

What wasn't taken from you
little vagabond. Your throat

is wrapped in a red scarf
like possessions in a nursery rhyme.

Sad clown, mime,
wise man from the east,

Edinburgh that is, waltzing
with a roll of linoleum.

I was your careless friend,
I didn't feed you, didn't call

and now you lie there
with a hole in your neck.

Jesus will personally greet you
at his front door, your painting

of the sauce bottles already on his
refrigerator. With nothing

but a bicycle and a guitar, your
whole life was a blue period.

Your stigmata scare me. Your nakedness
and your suffering are bad mannered.

How the Blue Nude Met the Demoiselles

The African masks were a decoy
a surface *sauvagerie*

and the encounter in a museum, how they trailed
their fresh magic like packing straw,

was a smokescreen. They were all bathers,
recycled Cezanne—a squatting thigh

an inviting armpit, but no up-draft here
no holy flame, no Toledo.

The melon's a cutlass. All the edges are sharp,
how we'll be lacerated

to heart flesh. Old friend, you went after
the blue nude like a dog

with a bone—checked the facts, the dates,
the outrage of Matisse, Mr. *Luxe*,

Mr. *Calme*. The shaggy brush work on the leg
and the sky color were stolen.

It was a thing with you to show what the little
plagiarist was up to.

Dear old blue nude, all of you weighs so much,
as if you're walking on Saturn,

bearing the heavy parts, and the young ladies, always
they beckon, always they bar the way.

The Tempest

Thomas Struth, the Dusseldorf school—my daughter
says on the phone, look them up online. I Google,
click, Google image, click, tumbling from one frame
to the next arriving at a photo in the Tate of an old
man at a table. She goes on—they were influenced

by the Bechers, but I'm in an eddy now, the old man,
Giles, the wallpaper, the architecture, *Edinburgh*
the text says, *Robertson*. I interrupt her, wait!
I know this man. I was in the room one evening
when chestnuts flowered on Saxe-Coburg Square.

He was an expert on the *Cinquecento*, gave us a lecture
on Titian's *Three Ages of Man* in the National Gallery
of Scotland, listing to one side like a monument about
to topple, his expression blissful, and on Giorgione's
Tempest. We stood within the atmosphere of awe

he cast after a lifetime devoted to its mystery—
the thunderclap, a broken column, the child suckling
oblivious, the mother naked in contrast to the clothed
man across the stream (light shines on his cod-piece,
not his face.) But just who is she looking at?

There was laughter, glasses clinked as Giles approached to say something witty, his gait swaying. He wore a ruby tie pin. We were braced by the proportions of the room, edified by the old masters. That would have been before the storm that placed us forever in one another's dreams.

National Library of Scotland

The National Library of Scotland was like an iceberg,
only one sixteenth of it showed above the surface;
or it was like one of those fungi with a relatively small
fruiting body and mycelia that go on for miles, knitting
whole fields together. We should have guessed, because
it took so long to get a book, especially the Iconography
of Cosmic Kingship by H.P. L'Orange, which came back
crypt-cool and old-smelling, so you could tell someone
had been down to the deep-delved earth, but when the fire
alarm went off, we finally had proof. There they were, mile
upon mile of troglodytic book people standing in a straggly
line past the People's Dispensary for Sick Animals where
you might see a German Shepherd with a bucket
round its neck, past the shop that sold prosthetic devices
in tan plastic—as if anyone in Edinburgh needed a tan
prosthesis—and all the way to the other bank. Indeed,
we could have guessed the size of it before because
George IV Bridge is actually a bridge, and you can peek
over the edge beside Baumeisters, where Escher-like
eighteenth century facades recede down to the Canongate
and you can gauge the fathoms of the NLS. Sometimes
we would catch sight of a book person, the chief of the book
people behind the Cerberus-headed librarian, but often not.
The noises of the others, their breaths, their footsteps

the squeaking of their little carts were all subsumed
into the purr of an air-handling machine which extracted
dampness out of every word ever written about Scotland.

Once on a cloudy day, shortly before tea-time an incident
occurred. I say on a cloudy day, because it was usually
a cloudy day and if not, then the acid etched roof glass
let in only hazy light, dulled further by chicken wire
embedded in the panels to ward off adventurous book thieves.
The muffling carpet was an orchid-lichen green, the color
of things that have a vicarious relationship to life and it did
nothing to remediate the gloom. The silence in the reading
room was so intense that you could hear ear-hair growing,
when suddenly a rock crashed through the ceiling, leaving
a neat little hole and landing with a thud on the dense
woolen carpet. Nobody looked up, but more remarkable
still, without any apparent stirring or sign of communication,
after an interval of three minutes, maybe less, a homunculus
appeared with a dust pan and brush and whisked the thing
away, as if he had been standing for years behind a panel
of fake books, waiting, on the off-chance that he should
have to retrieve an asteroid from the reading room floor.
After that there were no more irregularities, just our parting
on the mezzanine, your offering me help in perpetuity,
and my leaving you there, with the etched thistles
and jade terrazzo and the people who sweep away stardust.

Hacksilber

She brought all her suitors there
to see if they went with the scenery—the castle,
a river, the valley where the swan sleeps,

the place where Roman silver was discovered in 1919
some from Ravenna some from Constantinople,
an in-gathering of loot.

The grass was spongy from the high moss content.
They ran on it as children in their cable sweaters
and once a man looked out from a tower

to which there was no staircase.
Swans flew overhead and they photographed them
with a cine camera. She still has footage

of the huge and noisy wings. In the summertime
he came with her, which gave him an advantage—
willow leaves, pale and upside-down on the water.

Silver was thrust into the ground
leaving none to know the spot
wherein their wealth lay buried.

A Late Encounter with the Professor of Islamic Art

For no reason, I walk into a bookshop
and find you've written
the definitive edition on your subject
for Thames and Hudson.

Miles and years away
I see you at a window
the sun making silly leg shadows
on your safari trousers

and now you're a grey eminence.
Were the jokes for my benefit?
I know how I reveled
in our shared dislike of epic.

Of course I overlooked the thumb fungus
and your indecisiveness—
separating glass from coffee granules.
There was a coat of arms on all your books.

I stand before the shelf
and wonder whether I've been worthy
of that wink you gave me from the podium
in your red robe

and my heart curdles

even as I leave the shop with a bag

full of dawn over the mosque

and fondness rising like the doves of Cordoba.

Heavenly Ladder of John Klimax

The angels are outnumbered
out-maneuvered, dazzled
by each other's haloes.

They float in mid-air with their hands
modestly hidden
from God.

And how strong can the ladder be
with all those people on it
(none of them women

by the way.) It is such a precarious perch
and surely worm-eaten
by now.

If the devils were half as vigorous
there would be losses.
Then they simply

have better tools—lances, hawsers
arrows and they are nimble
unencumbered

by long robes. Getting off the top
rung is so awkward
you would think

that God might finally
reach down and
lend a hand.

Easter, New Jersey

The crocuses are forced.
A plastic loincloth flaps
on each tree. This is not

winter, this is not spring,
this is no season. Tollbooths
are stored by the turnpike

cherry-pickers also. At three
o'clock you dive off your
spring-board into oily water

contaminated with fluoro-
carbons, PCBs. Some sins
are as big as New Jersey.

There are no birds on the flats,
no hawks. The Cloisters
hold your carved ribs, ash

rungs for me to climb up.
All the way home, I drive
through the EZ Pass lane.

Reading Szymborska

She wears a scarf
smokes a cigarette.
Her words are gigantic
the space around them
wide as the Agora,
galactic winds
blow through each one.
She must write her poems
on a billboard
on the rooftop of an apartment
building at night
then reduce the lines
with the aid of a Xerox machine
to a millionth of the size
or boil them down
like cognac applesauce
until it holds its own
shape on a spoon.

From Russia

Your birth name
was odd, something
with *–evitch* missing

from the end
preserved on registrars
cream paper. Fling

with a tsar my fantasy
an inheritance of
exotic genes

comprehensive knowledge
of boar hunting
offspring who

see colored words.
How else could
I know the rhymes

of reindeer herders
or stride about the town
in Astrakhan—pelt

of involuted fetal curls.
I want to taste
the words again—samovar

from the summer
we had tea in glasses
cold salt potatoes.

Are there tunnels
in our deep
blood, can I confirm

that there were moths
in the pear orchard,
a lightning storm.

The Baptist

He roasts them
        on a makeshift hearth

and eats them hastily
        getting wings in his teeth—

their bodies are delicate
        and his fingertips too thick.

At noon he seeks a gully
        of moist sand, a rock overhang.

At sunrise he discerns sweetness
        and follows the bee.

He may spend hours carding
        camel hair, spinning it

on a staff of wood and clay.
        Stung by insects he is permeable.

In silence he sees straight roads
        on the curvature of the earth.

Shepherds

They were crude and toothless. They stank
and hoarded cheese in their pockets, affixed
weak lambs to themselves next to their skin.
On ragged and muffled feet they surrounded
us quietly. I was horribly exposed by firelight
to their curious eyes. There was shuffling
and confusion—I should have been terrified
for there had been rumors of bandits, but these
were mannerly people, quaint really, kneeling
and offering lambs. It was such a relief, to know
that we weren't alone in this strange escapade.

Syrian Grocer

Rose water, turmeric, boiled eggs in pink liquid
line the shelves of the Syrian grocer. A woman
rushes in, embraces an old man. The joy
of this re-union, is this an every day joy? Syllables
of a language I don't know cascade around them,
overflow, falling on the mint, the coriander.
The door to the store room is blocked by a man
with thick fingers talking on the phone. He's not
the proprietor, but exudes a sense of ownership
with his deep voice and polished shoes. Maybe
he is speaking Arabic. The proprietor is asked
to say something into the phone and does so
nervously. I wait at the counter while business takes
place looking at a picture of the Virgin and Child,
with more head ornament than is usual in western
iconography, a plastic clock with red plastic tomatoes
inscribed *Give us this day our daily bread* and sachets
of Greek mastic. A petite woman enters the store,
followed by an even smaller man, perhaps her father,
engulfed in army fatigues. They speak an African
language. Distinct consonants crowd the cash register,
the smiley face bags. The woman wears a floor length
denim skirt, a hat of arctic cammo fleece, like the
transparent wisps in Andy Warhol's late Last Suppers.
Languages pour from the re-united couple, the African

man and woman, the business associates. The grocers
are from Syria. I wonder how the war affects them as
I make my purchases. The owner serves me sheepishly.
The vowels of the woman in the fleece hat are beautiful.
Eventually I leave the store with her and with her father.
She turns to me and says Have a Nice Day (and all this
in slow motion) Jesus is Coming Soon. Maybe I hold the
door open for them. Maybe they hold the door open for me.

Henri Cartier-Bresson

I wish I were you Henri Cartier-Bresson
with your nimble ability and shuttered face.
You taped the metal parts of your camera
black for the barrio. Your eyes and mouth
don't belong together, your eyes belong
to another region, you are split as a Dutch
door. I wish I were you Henri Cartier Bresson
watching Matisse hold his dove's wings
and his doves on their various cages. I love
all the places you lived, I love your graph-
paper shirts, the hints of khaki, the pockets.
Quivering eel they called you for always
slipping away. You drank mint liqueurs
on the Rue des Moulins, cheeks the color
of shrimp. A gypsy predicted your sad Javanese
wife—some things you just can't make up.
You joined the resistance, escaped internment
on the third attempt, acquired fake papers
in Touraine. A witch doctor brought you
out of a coma when you almost died
of blackwater fever—there was a journey!
What reels you took and your mother's name
on cotton spools all over France. *Quel Blague!*
Threads tied you to everything—Ghandi's
last fifteen minutes—how uncanny. Some

things you just can't make up. I wish I were you,
Henri Cartier-Bresson, or had met you at the
Centre Pompidou, sketching on your shooting
stick, eyes attached to your heart, me on tiptoe.

Forefathers

They were flotsam and foundling. They took the baby
to Australia on a whim and had liaisons with a foreigner,
an archduke, a knife grinder or else they gave their prosaic
cuckoos Baltic names just for the heck of it. In Cyprus
or Syria they might abscond with an aristocrat, a fortune
teller and leave the other wet-eared brood to aberrant
stolid caretakers in the gene pool. Like balloon breasted
pigeons or drooling bulldogs they were bred to be odd,
to collect alpine flowers, antiquarian books, for beautiful
useless pass-times and always to be somewhere else—
Ayers Rock on a bicycle, the Pyramids in a Rolls Royce.
A word like *frangipani* could satisfy them all day.

The Oases

The oases were not as we expected,
wider, not pools in the dunes
clustered with date palms, but seasonal
rivers in the sand. I could have lived there
for ever closing runnels with an adze,
opening them to irrigate the coriander.
Do you remember how the mud brick
kept us warm at night without electricity
and the light came from palm nut oil lamps.
By noon, plots of clover were strewed
with shade and you photographed
the girls who ran across the spring wheat,
scarlets and pinks escaping from their robes.

Our Fiesta

If I lie on this bench a thought might fall to earth,
might twirl singularly, curled at the edges,
all its summer drained, trailing time in its wake
like the two of us in Seville, spinning
and making time. Had detectives followed us,
spied on us, they might not have heard the *saeta*
on the dark street, they might never have caught
the silhouette by the *Giralda.* Each scene
had a curtain sweeping the ground at our heels
and when we moved house they were quick
to dismantle the set. Within a week the market
was gone and the coffee shop, the storefronts
were empty. Oh, this is tricky, this talk of spinning,
of stage furniture and today in the newspaper
another metaphor, stirred molasses, to describe
the earth creating its own space-time. The imposters
may have gone to the same place, stayed in the same
hotel and eaten the same fish soup, but the saltimbanques
had taken off their flesh-toned hose, the gypsies
were asleep, because it was our fiesta, our sweet spoon.

Eastern Seaboard

Girls, Birds

I tell the delinquent girls anyway, about the warblers—
the magnolias and the parulas darting quickly
in the damp leaves, yellow and pointed and tropical.
They listen to me and talk through tongue studs,
their lycra abdomens bulge. The birds fly all the way
from the Caribbean, perhaps from Belize up to Canada
I tell them, to nest in the spruce forests, then back again.
I say "listen for high pitched songs." The girls smoke
hastily, for they are defenseless against this information
and they never suspected the world was surrounded by wings.

Cobb Hill Road, 1917

Beyond the brink of the road, heirloom
daffodils grow in bracken by the delicate
paths that deer have forged. Farther down
lie saucepans with the bottom rusted out,
the chassis of an old Ford. The day they tipped
it over with the handbrake off, gave it a big shove,
half a dozen village boys in collarless shirts
whooped to see it careen through brush
and flatten saplings. They inhaled the smell
of ravaged stalks, then celebrated with cold
root beer out of flagons. Water races past
that spot, year in year out, pale green,
the color of the silt the mountain makes.

Milledgeville

The quail, the mail-order swans, we are bird people
aren't we. I should like to have presented you
with a guinea fowl dear girl. I can see you maneuver
crutches to serve up Coca Cola and coffee mixtures
on the porch, also wicked good jokes, wise cracks.
No talk of form, only dog catcher, brick layer speech,
blunt and snarly and chained because there is nothing
clever to say in the face of the disease which eats mouthfuls
of chalk from your bones anonymously. Mother's rocking
chair was upholstered in the fur of an old fur coat—
a sort of dada rocker. I think of it now, along with
your devouring infirmity. Could we hum medieval hymns
together on your creaky chairs, the peacocks electric appearing.

Fireflies

We come downhill past Clark's farm
its high old maples above a bank of flowers
and they're emerging from the summer foliage
flashing semaphore in the last of the light.
You're transfixed, can't make sense of
what you're seeing, having no experience
of fireflies. I'm delighted at your wonder
because I planned the walk with this surprise
in mind. *You don't know how many people
I've described them to*, you say in hospital
your gaze so rapt, so far away, as if the first
impression of their sparkling is still with you
and we're in the same world at the same time.

The Metaphysicals

The Metaphysicals arrived last night and offered me a whiff
of ether from a demijohn. The silken hose of your life-force
are crinkled round the ankles they said, gesturing with floppy
cuffs. Come with us, we have ample equipment from which
to construct metaphors—sextants, mermaids, smiling cod
and the wiggly pink coastline of new continents. It sounded
interesting certainly, and for my part, I told them that a Swedish
lady at Harvard had stopped light, shone a beam into a tube
of very cold oil. A murmur of surprise went round the room
(John Donne is very cute, and Herbert has a pale moist brow.)
So earnest were they, holding skulls in monochrome, I was tempted
to go with them. How would I resist the man with the astrolabe.

Philadelphia

Look at your zig-zag chicken coop roofs and corrugated
Refinery roofs and oh, your dirty clerestoried wire-works.
Look! Bo's Rim shop, Elaine's Nail Shop and look at
your Rousseau chimney stacks. Your petite bourgeois
in their serge uniforms are gone now. Rusts and smuts bleed
down your highway bridges. The hawk dangles a snake.
On EconoLodge cable the bailbondsman's wife hires a dwarf
to wriggle on her husband's lap. The fat bride's waxy baby
pops out, the bride's mother cries. Nephews are waiting
by the swing doors. Your museum of surgery is full of safety
pins Philadelphia—many mothers breathed them in before
disposables. The children swallowed jacks and charms,
red beads and lead horses. There are dried corn kernels
and pistachio shells, all breathed in at one time. We eat corn-
hoe cakes and maple turkey sausage at the Terminal Market
and listen to Bad Moon Rising like in the Rousseau
at the Museum of Art. The revelers hold hands in the forest
as someone spies on them from a tool shed. Two nuns
buy relish from the Amish girls, zucchini and corn. The girls'
caps are white mesh, although they use a frankly tacky
and synthetic material for their dresses. There are marzipan
pigs for sale, chocolate guitars, ears or noses. No chocolate
noses in the museum of surgery, but molds of syphilitic
lesions and carbuncles and many diseases of the eye lid.
The bones of the inner ear are delicate and shell-shaped,

containing the sound of distant breakers. There's a naval
movie on TV. The ship's sails are beautiful, the ship surgeon
has beautiful instruments like the medieval spurs set on
butter-scotch walls in the Barnes Collection. I said Holy
Shit out loud in the Barnes Collection when I saw Cezanne's
bathers and Seurat's artist's studio, Matisse's lapises,
his odalisques, Van Gogh's sprig of spurge. Bristol
Meyers Squibb has a landscaped campus, smooth
as a golf course, except in the middle stands a dilapidated
house, covered with vines, grown vigorous in the mild
climate. I expect no-one could locate the owner, no-one
could find a deed in your court-house, Philadelphia.
It must have belonged to the unlucky one whose skull
is on display in the museum of surgery, or the dead lady
who turned into to soap when her fat reacted with lime
in the soil. She would bubble up after a good rainfall,
behind the tool shed, the rows of corn and the zucchini.

Mr. Elliot

Thank you Mr. Elliot, for your splendid life. I have spent
all morning with you on Great Spruce Head Island.
You looked beautiful and American, as if descended
from sea captains. Your skull was noble and you told me
that decay consumes. I imagine you spent days
on your belly in the rough grass, photographing sea birds
as the ocean merely lisped. The gentle adults
gave you a camera while your child fingers still plucked
berries in the reindeer moss. You knew the whereabouts
of steeplebush and meadowsweet. You admired ship
carpenters' houses, precisely mitred and of the Grecian style.
If only I had met you, I might have been content
to watch brine crystals form upon your arm, your eye
tethered to a wing. I might have packed you sandwiches
of lobster meat and sent you off to spend the afternoon alone.

Creatures and Beasts

It was a lean time, month of the hunger moon
the world run out of food, only a carcass from
beneath the snow to be picked clean. The grass
was flat and brown, wobbly with water, the hill
a jelly, turned out from the mold too soon. First
a turkey vulture came unfurling the black curtain
of its wings like a Victorian photographer, then
a fox appeared, nervous in the middle of the field
at noon. We looked out from the window, then snuck
behind the wood pile to watch the laborious
dismembering, one joint at a time until the bulk
could be dragged up to the tree line. He had a cache
somewhere was our guess from his intermittent
disappearances, half running with the heavy meat.
When he was done, late in the afternoon we walked
up to the crumbling wall and found the tail of a raccoon.

Fledged

In a crook of porch timber they built a nest of mud
and covered it in moss, the loose kind from the lawn
north of the maple tree. The hen became engulfed
in it so that we paid no heed until four mouths appeared
held up by small amounts of flesh. In one swift week
the nest contracted like a fist, so that the fledglings
had to flap their wings not to fall out. One by one
each made the momentous plunge, first to the arm
of a rocking chair, then the rim of a galosh and to a tree
behind the barn, some member of the dogwood family.
To our surprise a fifth appeared inside the nest. We willed
it on all afternoon, making our reports the way you do
a baseball game, but by the time it reached the rocker arm
the porch light was already on. When I checked before turning
in for the night it was on the boot, wide eyed and content.

Dear Mr. Butler

Please remove the everlasting light bulb.
It casts a sterile glow on your small plot of land.
Please also be informed that a thief can now insert
his crowbar into the seam of your doorjamb
without the aid of a Bic lighter. He need not trip
on the threshold as he removes your stereo equipment
nor tread on the tatters of moth wings. When I look down
on your cold square of illuminated asphalt Mr. Butler
I sigh and think—oh, how lonesome and pointless.
On autumn evenings a bright, unnatural mist
hangs over the entire valley, on account of your bulb
and all the time you are not there. Do you know
Mr. Butler that photons emitted from your light
have reached the constellation of Andromeda
where they believe you are the only god of a faded sun.

Indigo Bunting

That summer he was 89, sitting in an Adirondack
chair in the middle of the grass until he fell asleep
and it tipped him over on the ground when one leg
sunk into a divot made by Reggie Clark's cow.
A huge bruise covered the back of his hand
widening extravagantly because of blood thinners.
He never said a thing, but we noticed it at dinner.
Next day he was sitting in the same place more or less.
He came into the house full of wonder and asked
could it be that he had seen an all-over blue bird.

Gravity Fed

Maybe because I could hear the water all night
or because of the meat, what the cattle had eaten
herbs, fly agarics, I travelled the river in my dream
its peaty depths, recent spate-flattened margins,
took the falls at trout level, fearless. But even
before that, as I drifted off I was becoming
darkness around blackberries, black raspberries
as their juice chambers filled, dangling in gravity.
Was it the spring water I drank from a spigot
on the hillside that taught me things. In the morning,
sun lit the cartilage of your ear tips and the inside
of your T shirt sleeves from the east, salmon red
as you hauled water to water the tomatoes with
that walk of a farmer that your father had and
my thumb held a page in place against the breeze.

Morning

Frosted straw, wetted gold pasture grass in stripes
old leaves—I will pay any price for this
and one ounce of silence. I will pay any price
to see morning hang on the apple tree.
Preliminary air gathers in the valley's new time.
When they rise, heated draughts will bear the hawks
overhead, as far as the cloud margins. What do we
accumulate looking at quiet matter when it is sunlit.
My sinews are worshipful, my blood full of happy oxygen.

Green Valentine

Over-wintered apples sagged, oozing liquor.
Lime green parakeets, two escapees
from the tropics pecked at them, grew silly.
On Madison that day, two green parrots,
emerald in fact, were locked behind the grille
of an antique shop—some old emperor's good luck.
And what of us—charmed, chained or free
drunk on love in the wrong climate?

Dari-Joy

The world hangs in space like a bauble above
the Unitarian church altar where a woodwind trio
plays, followed by a string quartet. The violinist
and viola player stand up, swoop and dip to the music
as in the antic mating dance of cranes. The audience
is graying, eschews hair product, is in the madras
cotton phase of life, peers at eternity beyond
the horn of Africa, taken from a satellite. Our kids
don't want to hear Dvorak. They want ice cream
at the place that's open after 9:00 pm, so we cross
the bridge during intermission past Aumand's red
letters scrambled on the river to the blue neon
of the Dari-Joy. The mascot is a former BigBoy
with a quiff like chocolate soft serve, which sort of
qualifies him to be up on the roof. In the parking lot
there is a stench of toasted insects, so we go inside,
watch them dash themselves against the sign—
spring-tails, thrips, things that hatched out of water
are looping, frantic in the pastel light and there are
many, many, enormous black flies, mutant neon–
eating flies, all over the plate glass window which
reflects our mint chocolate chip with rainbow sprinkles,
monster sodas, giant plates of clam. A freight train
whistle blows and we hear the clank of cars going

to Canada full of bauxite and petroleum derivatives.
I suppose the Dvorak must be ending by the time
we drive back, see a fox in the stubble field,
then turn in the driveway and switch the one remaining
head lamp off, under the tree, under the milky-way.

About the Author

Audrey Henderson's writing is rooted in her early life on the edge of Edinburgh, Scotland, where the clash of city and country, ancient history and wrenching modern change began an enduring fascination with the interplay between the natural and the man-made environment.

She has been active in the areas of literacy and environmental education for the last ten years and is currently co-coordinating a school/church partnership and literacy volunteer program at an under-resourced Boston Public School. She is a long serving school program guide at the Arnold Arboretum of Harvard University.

Audrey graduated from the University of Edinburgh, She has written for BBC Radio Scotland and published a short story in the collection "Tales to Tell" which developed out of a radio series for schools.

Her poetry has appeared widely in both the United States and Britain, most recently in *Magma, New Writing Scotland 31, Tar River Poetry* and the *Midwest Quarterly*. She is the recipient of a 2014 Hawthornden Fellowship and was shortlisted for Scotland's Dr. Gavin Wallace Fellowship. She won second place in the River Styx International Poetry Contest and was a finalist in the Indiana Review ½ K Award as well as being chosen as a Special Merit Poet in the 2009 Muriel Craft Bailey Memorial Award Contest. She was a finalist the 2012 and 2014 Slapering Hol Chapbook Contests and the 2012 Philbrick Poetry Contest.

She lives in Boston with her husband Richard and their children, Helen and Emma.

HOMEBOUND PUBLICATIONS

At Homebound Publications we publish books written by soul-oriented individuals putting forth their works in an effort to restore depth, highlight truth, and improve the quality of living for their readers.

As an independent publisher we strive to ensure that "the mainstream is not the only stream." It is our intention to revive contemplative storytelling. Through our titles we aim to introduce new perspectives that will directly aid mankind in the trials we face at present as a global village.

At Homebound Publications we value authenticity and fresh ideas. From the submissions process where we choose our projects, through the editing phase, the design and layout, right to the crafting of each finished book, our focus is to produce a reading experience that will change the lives of our patrons. So often in this age of commerce, entertainment supersedes growth; books of lesser integrity but higher marketability are chosen over those with much-needed truth but a smaller audience. We focus on the quality of the truth and insight present within a project before any other considerations.

WWW.HOMEBOUNDPUBLICATIONS.COM